1

The Black Book of Spiritual Secrets

Vol.1

ISBN 978-1-105-81304-7

Introduction

I did not create a table of contents for this book because the entire book should be read from beginning to end. This is some of the most important information that you will ever read, so take your time and enjoy.

The book of genesis is one of the most well-known, yet misunderstood books of our time. In the beginning God created the earth out of a formless void of darkness. I had never seen the creation in the manner that I'm about to describe until I met my former teacher. No one really knows how, when or even if God really created the earth, universe or human beings. I've always found it fascinating how many preachers would preach the creation of everything as if they were really there when it happened. When they are confronted with competing theories, they immediately begin to attack the new source of information. With that said, let's use the bibles own words to explain the situation.

Genesis tells us that God created the earth, and after its creation it was formless and void, and covered in deep darkness. According to the consistent usage of the phrase "darkness" in the bible (such as Isaiah 60:2) darkness is used to describe a condition of spiritual ignorance or wickedness. Rarely does it ever mean the absence of the energy of light. From reading the Gnostic texts, we were taught a great deal about spiritual light and darkness. The bible touches on this issue, but it doesn't clearly define the origins of the two entities; for this reason the Gnostic text better explains the true nature of light and darkness. It took me some time to realize that the bible is one big parable about Jesus Christ. The harlot churches are too concerned with trying to explain every little story in the bible, instead of giving the spiritual meanings and interpretations. This understanding would be easier to come by if church members were actually allowed to do their own research and study the way they desire to study. Most Christians have never read a single Gnostic document from either the Nag Hamadi or the Dead Sea Scrolls. For them, this is foolishness. I can't express the importance of learning what the people before you thought and believed. Creation didn't make any since to me prior to meeting the teacher, but after that experience I began to see things more clearly. This earth is very old, and so are its inhabitants. From placing together different sources of the creation story, it appears that God created a planet similar to the many other planets in our universe. After this planet was created it was placed on the outer edges of creation which is known as time. After the earth was placed in its place, there was a heavenly host of beings assigned to form the earth and its spiritual condition. It is beyond me why this sounds like heresy to many Christians, because the same process is going on today. Humans have been given control over the production and development of the world. Our societies are designed by the ideas of the human mind. Everything from the architectural layouts of our cities, to the education systems are the product of the human mind. What we don't see is how spiritual beings have direct influence over the behavior of the humans on earth. When Adam and Eve arrived on earth they were given instructions to be fruitful and multiply, as well as to subdue the earth. There was also a counsel of beings located in the "garden of Eden" to give Adam and Eve instruction and guidance. At the arrival of Adam and Eve there were already beings on the earth living in other areas surrounding the garden. Theses beings are what we know as primitive man. In the Gnostic text of the gospel of Phillip, we can see that humans are prone to having animal like instincts until they receive the spirit of God. This is largely due to the fact that the evil spirits that govern the world are not human in nature, they are animal-like. These spirits are attempting to keep humans under the influence of animal like behavior instead of a human-like nature. In the book of Daniel we read that God had taken the human spirit from King Nebuchadnezzar, and given him an animal spirit. Without God, humans are nothing more than animals. The animal nature is that which desires to have uncontrollable sex, eat unreasonable portions of red meat, and dominate our neighbors completely in order to make them fit into our purposes. This is what the beings were like on the earth at the arrival of Adam and Eve. Despite what many people may believe, humans were never meant to multiply at the rate in which we have. This is largely the result of our inability to control our bodies. It is said to believe that Adam and Eve were spiritual beings upon their arrival, but they put on human flesh to spiritually subdue the inhabitants of the earth. They failed at this mission because they could not control the flesh they inhabited. They gave in to sexual perversion and lost their positions as leaders of the earth. After they sinned against God, the heavenly counsel left Adam and Eve to their own devices. This meant that they were now under the leadership of the Luciferian regime. They had become a part of the "world" system. Adam and Eve were not born of the world in the sense that they had earthly parents. They were in fact, created from the earth. Their bodies had no genetic tie to the inhabitants of the earth, but that changed after Eve got impregnated with the seed of the world. Adam and Eve were not new creations, but they were celestial messengers sent to this planet to fulfill a divine mission. It is very possible that the beings of the earth were nothing more than evolved animals until they united with the divine seed of God's messengers. This theory repeats itself throughout the Old Testament stories of the Nephilim, and all of the regulation forbidding Hebrews from marrying other nationalities. The bible is very clear on the fact that God's messengers are never to marry those who are not. God had sent his people in as strangers, and they became locals. They became one of the members of the world. Since that time God has sent numerous messengers and prophets to the earth to prepare the way of righteousness. The difference is that these beings were the children of sexual intercourse so they themselves weren't holy, but their message was. This is the basis of all of creation as far as it pertains to the earthly existence. One must not confuse the physical creation with the spiritual creation. This was an entirely different event all together. In fact, spirits were created well before the world was. Spirits are eternal. This means that once they are created they will live forever. We too often forget that eternal does not mean infinite, which is what God is. Infinite means always existing from beginning to end. God created spirits out the same substance as the Godhead. The father took eternity and infinity out of him and created the son. The son took infinity out of him and created the Holy Spirit. They all are infinite in their nature due to the fact that they never separated from the original source which is the father. In a fleshly comparison you can say that they are similar to clones of each other, except they are only clones in nature. Human spirits, or the spirits that came to occupy human bodies, were created from the same substance as the godhead. The godhead is spirit and love, and so are human spirits created. The difference is that human spirits are not aware of themselves. They are ignorant of their true nature. Spirits are empty except for a few built in programs that will allow them to eventually find their source. This is a part of the curse that was placed upon Adam and Eve. Our spiritual ancestors were aware of their nature to a large degree, but their sin blinded them to the totality of their existence. As a result of this, human beings were created ignorant of their nature and origin. Some spirits were aware of themselves before entering into this realm, but they lost their information upon entering into this dimension. These beings are commonly referred to as angels or messengers. In fact, some human beings are indeed angels according to the spirit. At some point God gave these angels missions to come to the earth for a specific purpose and assignment. In most cases it is to collect souls, which are the blank spirits that are in the world. In some Gnostic text the souls are called the images of the angels. This means that the souls of the individuals are molded after the form of their angelic teachers or ministers. I'm not sure what Adam and Eve were spiritually, but they could have been extremely high celestial beings. Understand that when I speak of missions I am not referring to angel having conversation with the creator. What this means is that these spirits were programmed to function a certain way, without the spirit even being aware of it. This is why the notion of free will is an illusion. Nowhere in scripture do we read WHY God created humanity. This is the mystery of scripture. The bible purposefully doesn't mention the missions of humans being on earth because it is the goal of the individual to discover his individual life's purposes. This is part of the reason why I find it so strange how preachers talk about this issue as if they know for certain. They speak in terms of concrete truth when it's all assumption. What I believe is that every spirit (or person) is on earth for different reasons. The earth isn't an exception to the rule of creation, it IS the rule. Everything has its own unique purpose, and that also means people. I don't pretend to know the fate of the people around me, but I am aware that many of them are nothing more than occupied vessels. The battles of the heavens are going on right now on earth within the social conflicts of society. It is no coincidence that we live in a world that cannot seem to ever remain in a state of peace. It is no coincidence that humanity has a history of treating each other as less than human. All of these are the result of a world that is filled with vessels of light, vessels of darkness and vessels of uncertain future. We are playing roles in a movie of divine importance. The bible talks vividly about the salvation of souls as being the most important reason for existence. One must not confuse the salvation of souls with the salvation of mankind. Mankind is not souls in general. Many members of mankind are indeed filled with spirits of darkness. It doesn't matter how one feels about the notion of demons, devils and such. What is important is that you know that they are real. Whether you see them as creations of Satan or some type of metaphor it really doesn't matter. When they occupy human bodies they are the enemy of enlightenment. Human fear has created a plethora of dark spirits that now reside within our realm. Fear is the most powerful negative energy, just as love is the most powerful energy period. When we fear anything, we are creating dark spirits that take on the role of demons in our world. In fact our world is designed to perpetuate fear because it is ruled by the king of fear- Satan. Human beings are taught to fear things that are different, whether it is skin color, language or even death, the human nature is to fear the unknown. This powerful force maintains the existence of the world and the universe. Have you noticed how mankind has continued to find that there are more and more planets in our universe? It almost seems that the longer we live, the more the alien planets manifest themselves. The vastness of outer space seems to only get bigger and bigger as time moves along. This directly reflects mankind's relationship with God. The more man feels that he is self-sufficient without God; the more planets get between us and the highest heaven. We are slowly building a prison around ourselves through our fear of death. This was a part of the reason why the spirits of Adam and Eve were sent to this planet. The creator knew that man was building an entire creation out of fear, and these two celestial messengers were sent to inform the earth's inhabitants of the truth. This was the original attempt to stop the building of the tower of babel. Man constructs worlds out of his fear of leaving the material existence, but he has yet to realize that he is going to die anyway. Nothing can stop that from happening. It is similar to how people build bomb shelters to survive nuclear war and radioactive fallout, but if it ever does happen the radiation will kill them eventually anyway. It is a stubborn foolishness to hold on to that which passes away. The creation of matter and illusion is not of God. This is the result of man's fear of separation and loss. If this world was the creation of the almighty, why would it pass away? The mind of man came to realize its individuality so it had to create somewhere to live, as a result it created this prison. Now it is afraid to leave here because it doesn't know what else is out there. Despite the teachings of the church, this was not the result of Adams sin; it was going to happen anyway. The result of his sin is ignorance of our true origin. He had forgotten where he had come from and started to believe that he was of this world. This is why Christ came to the earth; to gather the celestial spirits into the arc of knowledge and salvation. For the descendants of the wicked that lived on the earth prior to Adam and Eve's arrival, nothing good awaits them because they are deformed and disembodied spirits at their core. They have chosen to live in eternal darkness. That's the sad truth for many people around the world. It sounds like some type of racist or prejudicial comment, but the fact remains that many people are nothing more than pawns on a chest board. Their nature is wickedness and darkness. Their spirits are not those of "normal" people. I won't get into it too much in this now but I may discuss it later. After the failure of Adam and Eve in their mission to enlighten the beast people of the earth about the true ways of God, they forgot who they were and what they had come to this earth for. Since that time many celestial spirits have been born into bodies of earth with no knowledge of who they really are. They parade around the world as if they are at home, when in fact they are nothing more than missionaries or pilgrims. They have drunk the cool-aide of delusion and drank the wine of the wrath of God. When the bible says that God is not willing that any should perish, it speaks of the celestial spirits and souls that journey into this realm, not the seeds of darkness. This is quite difficult for people to understand because they have a false sense of "what" God is. Remember that this world is a battleground so there must be two sides of the war.

I previously mentioned that people have a misunderstanding as to what God is. This is largely the case because people have been improperly taught by church leaders that God has the same personality traits as human beings. This is how politicians can feel that God actually cares about who wins an election. This is why athletes feel that they can pray to God for a victory over their opponent. Only rational and partial beings can hold a favorite horse in a race. Unfortunately this is the box that people have also placed God into. In order to correct these misunderstandings we have to first address the origin of the confusion; this lies with the notion that God is in fact "a God." The kolbrin bible states that the unknowable, unreachable being has been called "God" by mankind out of our simplicity. In fact, many believe that god was a plural form before modern language made it singular. This means that god was never spoken of as one, but one of many. Many mythologies around the world speak of multiple gods in the creation of the world. The bible speaks of Elohim (plural) creating all of creation. It wasn't until the modern church was formed that the word god was taken to represent the one divine being. If you study the word god, you'll notice that a singular god was only responsible for a small fraction of the creation process. Other aspects of creation were created by other types of gods. In its original context, god was never an omnipotent, omniscient, omnipresent being. He was nothing more than a being of special abilities over a particular element. God, in this context, is nothing more than an idol. He is an external being that is there to control particular elements in our lives. This is where people get the idea that god is supposed to perform in a manner similar to a genie. They make their demands (prayer) and their god is supposed to grant them whatever they ask for. This is the nature of the idea of a god. It's because of our ignorance that we fail to see the truth of our identities as spirits, and our creator as the one true spirit. The King James Bible does not mention god as being the Spirit of all spirits. In order to see this portrayal one would have to read the apocryphal texts. In these writings, God is called the "Lord of Spirits." It was understood that the Creator of spirits must be a spirit himself. In fact, he IS spirit. He was never meant to be lessened to the status of a god. In earlier times lesser spirits operated in the role of gods. The fallen messengers of the book of genesis were considered to be the gods of the pre-flood world. Satan is said to be a messenger and also the god of this world. In the occult book known as the Oahspe, the angels that created the different levels of the heavens and the hells were functioning as gods in the world, but they were not the creator. If humanity is to excel beyond this current level of ignorance, we must first get over this notion that the most high is a god, or the God. Gods are objects of worship, whereas the Most High wants not worship, but union with Him. It is this absurdity in the teaching that He is a god that allows people to believe that there is some heaven that awaits them no matter how hellish they choose to live on this earth. Churches are filled to capacity with people who live double lives. The first life is the one that everyone sees when they are out in a public place such as church, and the other is their perverted and dark interior life. They figure that if they do all of the right things in front of the right people that they will hold a high status in church and religious society. They feel that they will be forgiven of all of their wickedness because their pastor says that god is love. They make no effort to know the truth, or to be known BY the truth. Jesus said that ye shall KNOW the truth and the truth shall set you free. The bible talks about people that say Lord, Lord, but he never knew them. To be known by the Most High is the most important thing that one can obtain in this life. But it is impossible to be known by him if you hold a false idea of what he really is. He is not the idol that society has created within the illusionary realm of their minds. He is not the image painted in the cathedrals of Europe. Above all, he is not a God. Gods are nothing more than messengers who have adopted a personal ego of self-importance. The bible says that The Most High is word. Because he is word, his "angels" are messengers of His words. We are to listen to his words that are spoken through his messengers, and become that message. Once we become that message, we take on the nature of the Creator Himself, thus becoming His sons. (Whether we know it or not, we are constantly relaying some type of message.) This transformation takes us into the kingdom of God. Psalms 82:6 says that we are gods. The angelic beings of scripture are messengers of a particular attribute of what is known as the godhead. Because of our position, we are able to ascend beyond their ranking into the role of gods. This only sounds blasphemous to someone who still believes that The Most High is Himself, a god. If you know that He is not a god, but something much, much higher, there would be no offense in that statement. The creator is extending Himself, and His family. With the modern understanding of salvation, we are simply waiting around for rapture from a god, who wants to nothing more than to give us things. This coincides with the teaching that we are a helpless creation waiting for redemption from an external god. It is this way of believing that is the result of Adam and Eve's fall. We have forgotten that we are messengers of the Almighty, and we've chosen to become victims of our environment. We have become products of this farce of a world. In short, we are now OF the world. Do not fall for the lie that the Almighty intended for life to be this way, because He didn't. The problems of this life are created by the perversions of mind. This world is the creation of thought and will, not of the Most High. Humanity is the reflection of the dark forces that existed prior to the arrival of Adam and Eve. Our spiritual predecessors failed to teach and convert the fallen species into the way of the Most High. Because of this, we are now a reflection of that failure. It is up to us to turn away from that failed nature and to return to our previous state of being. The Almighty has shown us the way out of darkness through the life of Yeshua Messiah. If you are still waiting for a god to save you, you will be waiting for a while. It is the expectation of an external god that will cause humanity to worship the son of perdition. Our father has given us the keys to the kingdom through his lamb, and the angelic messengers.

The return to our previous state is the goal of all of the celestial being incarnated within this realm. In order to complete this process, one must acknowledge that we have an origin somewhere other than this world. This can be rather hard to grasp by those who still believe that they are serving a god instead of the Lord of Spirits. If you feel that you were created from the dust of the earth, and that your existence started once you were born, you will remain in darkness. It is close to impossible to return back to your previous state if you are serving an external god. It is this perspective that leads many to believe that the Lord is just sitting around waiting to pound them with judgment. It is this external perspective that forces people to think that they can somehow convince God of their righteousness. They believe that they can have a conversation with God, and that He will weigh their good deeds against their bad deeds, and all will be forgiven. The bible says that men will reap whatever they sow. It also says that The Almighty is no respecter of persons. In other words, He has no favorites. Jesus spoke of the closeness of the kingdom of heaven, even during His day. The apostles went to their deaths with a certainty in what they were dying for. The bible says that if we ask we shall receive, and that we will find if we seek. These promises were not meant to be fulfilled at death, but while we are in our bodies. To enter the kingdom of heaven is to be found deep within our being. This realm is beyond the body, the mind and even the soul. It is the highest level of existence. It's returning to the highest source of love and knowledge. It's returning back to the Father. When all flesh is removed, the real you remain. This is what the early mystics understood, but the believers have forgotten today. Teresa of Avila called it the interior castle. Inside of this castle, Teresa taught that there were a number of interior spiritual dwelling places. Our ascension is literally inward. The bible speaks of new wine inside of old wine skins, and treasures in earthen vessels. Both of these parables refer to the spirit inside of the vessel, and not on the outside. It is actually a sin to seek the Lord anywhere but inside of the temple, which is the body. This includes the search for an external heaven. I'm not denying the existence of an external heaven, but I AM saying that it is a reward given to those who have been born of the spirit. In the book of Job we read that in my flesh I shall see god. It is this knowledge that opens the internal spirit of man. There is no need to wait until death to find your way back to the Almighty. Beyond our flesh, mind, will and emotions lay that piece of eternity that was sent from the Father. Unless that part is born again within the flesh, it will go to a hellish existence after the death of the body. This is why Jesus' message was so urgent. Death lays at the door for everyone, and no one knows exactly when it is coming. If the true spirit dies in ignorance it cannot go back to the origin of creation which is the Almighty. It is not clean enough to enter that realm, so it will wonder between realms forever. It's all about the awareness of the internal existence. Bernard of Clairvaux put it best when he said "he who does not come to the knowledge of himself before the death of the body will be trapped within himself forever". There are two existences that every human being must contend with. The first is the pre-birth, pre-body existence. This is the true self that existed with the Father before you were conceived or born. The second is the body/material existence. This is the personality that is developed through the mind, ego, and body experiences. It is this affiliation that hinders many people from ascending back to the Father. It is impossible to make the ascension if you are attached to the life of this realm. It is very difficult to leave behind family and friends when your personal identity is attached to these people. This fear is a form of spiritual handcuff that keeps everyone bound to the realms of shapes and images or form. The fear that we face is designed by the forces of this realm to keep people focused on the issues of this realm. Emotions are unique to the life in the body, not the life beyond. The Father is waiting for his spirits to awaken to their true nature, and return to their Father for instruction and guidance. Spiritual ascension is not a matter of faith; it's a matter of knowing. The bible says that faith is the substance of things hoped for, the evidence of things not seen. Faith is the basis and foundation of our relationship with the Almighty. We need it to accept the reality of our existence. Once we accept the reality of our existence, we no longer need faith because we will come to know the truth. At this point we are operating with patience. Patience is the substance of the present moment. It doesn't survive dwelling on the past, nor does it need to fantasize about the future. It's understanding that all we need is given to us in the present moment-the I AM. The ascension of the spirit is accomplished after proper spiritual garments have been acquired. Don't get confused, the awakening is the most important part, but this is not complete ascension. To ascend one must master the usage of forms. It's a complete mastery of all of the potential of the spirit, without affiliating yourself with any given form. Many people believe that Jesus only appeared on this earth as the child of Mary and Joseph. But the reality is that the Spirit of God (Jesus) appeared many different times, using many different forms. Prior to His incarnation in the birth body, the Spirit of God manifested Himself as He so desired. These manifestations were not only done in our realm of visibility, but in many other dimensions as well. He was able to accomplish this because of His nature.   After His birth and crucifixion in the flesh, He gave us all a way back into that knowledge and power. Through this doorway that He opened, all of the Father's celestial spirits now have the keys to the nature of God. Remember, the Father is not a god, but He's so much more. Godliness and the divine nature are given to us as a gift of our awakening. Outside of the manifestation of the Almighty Father, all that exist is God. Within the title of God there are particular attributes and virtues that must be attained. In order for a spirit to ascend into God, it has to be adorned with all of the Godly virtues of divinity. These virtues can only be obtained through a lifetime in the flesh. Because there are certain lessons that can only be learned through experience, the celestial beings of the Father must overcome the temptation to associate identity to the flesh or any other form. To know ones self is to know that you are nothing without your union with the Almighty.   Once you know this, (not believe, but know) you have overcome the lure of the flesh.   Just as Adam was sent to this realm to teach spirits and souls how to come back to the Almighty, the second Adam came to call lost spirits back to their origin.   But in order for this process to be completed people must first come to the knowledge of the true self, and secondly, be transformed into the virtues of God. Not everyone will succeed in this task, as we all know. Some will fail and not enter into the kingdom but go somewhere else. Aside from this, only those who are completely transformed will ascend. This is why angels in the higher dimensions cannot obtain that level of Godhood. Because angelic messengers can only represent one divine attribute, it is impossible for them to obtain all of the divine virtues. It's a matter of being not believing. This transformation is one of the greatest mysteries of scripture. No one can expect to ascend if they don't know what they are ascending to. The confusion of the church is rooted in the belief that we are trying to "make it" into heaven, and not return to it. This notion is perpetuated by the belief that the human spirit is going to leave the earth to live somewhere else.

Heaven has been one of the most confusing topics since the beginning of time. For different religions and different cultures, the place of divine rest has different interpretations and different meanings. No one knows what the nature of the next life will be, so we continue to speculate about its nature. I'm going to take the scripture from the book of revelation in the bible that says there will be a new heaven and a new earth. In order for there to be something "new" there has to be something old. From what we can gather from this notion is that there is or was a heaven that previously existed, and in the future there is going to be something "different." we all know what the current earth is, so it doesn't take much revelation or speculation to figure out its nature. The earth hasn't changed much since its creation, but the inhabitants of the earth have had their influence on its destruction. The earth is a living being and it goes through the cycles of life and death, just as humanity. These cycles are billions of years apart, but they do occur. This process of death can be expedited by deterioration of the spiritual conditions of its inhabitants. When the people of the earth are in proper relationship with the Almighty, the earth will have a long and prosperous life. When the earth's inhabitants are in a state of spiritual unconsciousness, the earth will start to die at a much faster rate. When this death occurs there will be an increase in natural disasters, wars and pestilences. The culmination of this death is recorded vividly in the bible and the Kolbrin. When the earth starts to die, the inhabitants won't stand a chance at survival. In essence, death of the earth is death to mankind. The New Age movement claims that people are becoming more enlightened, but it may be too late. The destruction of the earth is at hand, and the wheels are already set into motion. This current society will not survive. The vast majority of the earth's social structure will be destroyed at some point in the future, whether sooner or later, it doesn't matter. This is what prophets have been screaming about for years, and people have failed to heed the warnings. Instead of changing, the religious people of the world have sat quietly and waited for its end. They preach of dooms day and Armageddon, but they fail to realize its causes. They fail to realize that humanity's spiritual ignorance is the cause of these catastrophic events. They say that its Gods judgment on the wicked, but they never consider the fact that they could very well be a part of that same wickedness. Human beings have turned into self-centered beasts who want nothing more than to fulfill their selfish desires for wealth, power and sex. No consideration is being paid to the inner man. It is all about living in the pleasures of the moment, which provide temporary satisfaction for the empty vessels that inhabit the planet. This lack of attention to the inner man is due to the fact that people aren't aware of the fact that the entrance into heaven is on the inside of them. Because there is a belief that heaven is only external, human beings turn their attention to the things that are external to themselves. They feel that they need to gather external things in order to feel complete. This leads people to believe that the answer to their internal emptiness is found in the world around them. This belief causes human beings to attach themselves to the things of this world. For those who feel that money and sex are the greatest pleasures in this world, they lack the ability to understand that there are far greater experiences inside of their true being.

Heaven is presented to be "out there" and not in here. The Gnostics believed that knowledge of reality was the way to salvation. Because their teachings are all but outlawed by the modern church, most people will never know the value of their perspectives. To know something is far more powerful than it is to believe something. Belief is the basis of today's church. There is very little that they can claim to know for certain. This lack of knowledge is the basis for the death of the Almighty's people. The bible says that the Lord's people perish for a lack of knowledge; it did not say that they perish for a lack of belief. Don't get it confused, faith is NOT belief. To have faith, we have to know exactly what it is that we have faith in. I don't have to believe that it's cold outside; this is something that I can know for certain. The same thing applies to salvation and heaven. As long as we are trying to find

42

something to "believe" in, we will never know the truth. It is this fundamental principal that the Gnostics held. So what exactly can we know about heaven? First of all, we can know that it is a state of perfect understanding of our being. There would be no questions about our existence in any place called heaven. Secondly, we know that heaven would be a state of no pain; emotional or physical. Pain is a distraction from the truth of the present moment. Lastly, heaven would be a state of forever being in the Lord's presence. We cannot have the other things if we are separated from the Lord. This reality is fully attainable in the state of complete consciousness, and apart from a body of limitation. Most people do not understand how much reality is blocked through the illusion of their bodies. For the spiritually asleep, it's hard to imagine life without a body;

this is the reason why heaven is always viewed as a place instead of a state of being.

Heaven is only seen by those who are spiritually awakened while in this body. Without physical eyes it is impossible to see anything that is external. Because of this, one has to be awakend with the internal eyes of the spirit. The Nag Hamadi mentions that the "physical" world is only a reflection of the spiritual reality. There is an entire universe that exists within the spiritual consciousness. To be conscious is to be aware of the truth. Once this awareness is awakened, then we are able to see things as they truly are. The Lord does not send anyone to heaven or hell; He simply created the rules of the game. Your final destination is determined by the level of spiritual enlightenment that you allow yourself to obtain while in this body. This is why the bible says that God will not be mocked. For all of those who seek understanding and knowledge on this earth, they will find the Kingdom of Heaven. This goes back to what I mentioned about spiritual transformation. Once you have been transformed into the likeness of God, you will have entered the kingdom of Heaven. I have done quite a bit of studying on the nature of the universe and the nature of the spirit. The external universe that we are able to see is an illusion -a reflection of the Lord's true kingdom. It is created and maintained by spirits of darkness that exalted themselves in order to be worshiped as gods. Nothing good can come from the formed universe of our current state of existence. Scientists are fooling themselves into believing that there is great knowledge to be found in studying the stars of our universe. They hold on to foolish hopes of finding a new home for the human species. This is the root of the fascination with "earth-like" planets. The truth is that the human creature on earth will never live there. The goal of the spiritual entities that control this dimension is to keep men looking outward and not inward. These entities cannot enter into your inward life unless you invite them, so they manipulate the world around you to get you to turn your attention to their power. Once these entities are able to enter into your inner dimension, their lives will be short and violent due to the presence of the Most High. They are trying to use mankind to find their way back into the Lord's presence because they have been locked out of that realm. They are forced to live an existence that is bound to the physical world. The universe around us is in one form or another version of hell. For all of those who believe in extraterrestrial visitors, you must know that if you have seen one of them, they are demonic. The kingdom of heaven is not visible to human eyes. This is the reason why the bible says that eyes have not seen, ears have not heard, nor have minds conceive what God has prepared for those who love him. The next realm is beyond the scope of our reasoning. I like to liken it to as Eckhart Tolle says "the inner space." There are multiple dimensions within the known universe, just as it is with the inner universe. Inside of every human being has the ability to access the kingdom of heaven. It is, however, impossible to enter into this kingdom without the second birth-the birth of the inner consciousness. For those who have not been born again, this notion seems quite similar to the New Age or occult philosophies. The idea that the portal to heaven is on the inside of the individual takes away the status of the modern-day preacher. You don't need someone to preach to you every Sunday in order to enter into the kingdom. As a matter of fact, if you have not entered into the kingdom prior to death, you will definitely not enter into it after you die. It is possible to know where you are going before you leave this body, but if you have not received the second birth your understanding will be cluttered. The Holy Spirit is heaven itself. Once you receive the Spirit, you will begin to develop a hunger for the deeper things of the Lord. This hunger will lead you to search high and low to find answers to your inner questions. If you search diligently, you will find the answers. An accurate search will lead you to enter into the inner universe.

The inner universe is quite different from the outer universe. For one, the inner universe contains realms (dimensions) that are completely habitable. Within our visible universe there are billions of planets of death. They are lifeless voids of darkness. It is very likely that scientist will never find true life on other planets, because our universe is dying. We see that there are tons of planets that will never be habitable by the human creature. Life will not be extended through the valley of death that we call our universe. The pure nature of our universe is darkness. The only light within our cosmos are the stars and planets. Without them, we would have nothing but darkness. The inner space is a universe of light. The inner universe is one planet with different realms. The interior universe does not have voids and boundaries such as our exterior universe. Its many levels are accessible through spiritual development and knowledge. It is open to people who have achieved a particular level of enlightenment while on the earth, and if a person hasn't completely developed while inside of the material body, they will be given an opportunity to do so in that realm. It's vastly different from the image of reality that we call our universe. But be warned, if a person ignores the voice of God while in this body, they will not be given an opportunity to grow. They will be annihilated. Because we are physical beings, we have physical limitations. Once we leave this body, we will become conscious or spirit beings and we will only be limited by our lack of consciousness and sprit. The Lord is fair to everyone. What you choose to learn while in this body is completely up to you. If you deny the truth of the Lord, you will suffer the consequences by sending your consciousness into an unconscious hell. The bible says that this current heaven and earth will pass away, and that there will be a new heaven and a new earth. It also tells us that there will be a unity between the Almighty and man. After the heavens depart away as a scroll, all will be left is the Lord's presence. This is the new heaven AND the new earth. There will no longer be a separation between the two realms because it is the sin known as the flesh that currently separates us from God. The Gnostics believed that all matter was bad. I understand the premise behind that, but I believe that matter itself isn't bad, only when it is unchecked by the spirit of truth. When matter is allowed to run amuck, it goes about creating prisons for the spirit consciousness. These prisons are known as the things of this world, or more matter. It creates more and more illusions to keep the spirit man dumb and ignorant to the life within. Matter cannot create spiritual or interior reality, so it has to continue to create externally. This is Satan exalting himself to be equal with the Most High's throne. I once read that "Satan" is translated as the "flesh." The flesh, or Satan, wars against the true kingdom of heaven, which is planted inside of man. This battle has been going on since the beginning of humanity. To truly overcome Satan is to overcome the will of the body. The flesh wants more of itself, and the same goes for the spirit. Man has access to both heaven and hell at all times. If you choose to live according to the inner man instead of the flesh, you will see the true kingdom of God. The difficulty in seeing the kingdom of heaven comes from the fact that we are forced to filter everything through the veil of the body. To overcome Satan IS to overcome the desires of the body. The mind of man uses the body to carry out its desires. The body is a dumb entity because it is only able to do what the mind or the spirit tells it to do. For all of those who follow the way of the flesh, they will dwell in everlasting darkness, or ignorance.

As of the resurrection of Jesus, lost spirits wander from dark realm to dark realm, hoping to find some type of direction. Until the final judgment happens to our universe, these spirits can dwell in any number of hell universes or dimensions. But once this current system of heaven and earth separation is done away with, they will have nowhere to go but outer darkness.

As time rolls along, we are starting to see that humanity is becoming less religious and more spiritual. As a result of this spiritual awakening there are more and more people publishing works on the nature of the spirit. When I was first introduced to the notion that the spirit and the body were separate beings, I found as many resources as I could on the topic. The task was quite daunting because there are so many writings that have been published on the issue. If you've ever done this type of research, you may have noticed an increase in the number of people that believe that the mind is the true spirit of man. For decades we have been told that man is a triune being; containing a mind, body, and a soul. The soul was never really defined, but the mind has now become the focus of our attention. But what exactly is the mind? Is it really a part of the divine nature? In order to answer these questions we have to examine the true attributes of the mind itself.

For most people the mind is an uncontrollable entity that fights to control the body. They believe that it is much better to have the mind control the body, than it is for the body to have free reign over itself. This would be true if the person really had control over their mind. We have seen that the mind has a very difficult time staying focused on the tasks at hand. Too often does the mind drift into the future, or wander back into the past. The mind is a very active being that needs someone to control it.

The underlining message of the scriptures is to not only control the body, but to also put the mind into submission as well. The bible says that we are to bring every thought into the obedience of Christ. In order to get the full meaning of this text, we have to first understand who Christ is, and how do we obey him. If you are someone who believes that Christ was one man who lived over 2000 years ago, then you will have a difficult time understanding the depth of this scripture. Christ is the Spirit that was inside of the man known as Yeshua Ben Yousef, or Jesus, the son of Joseph. The creator cannot be born, and he has no mother or father. The man Jesus was called the lamb, not the Christ. The bible clearly mentions two beings in the book of revelation; the lamb, and the son. The son occupied the lamb in order to make it holy. Once the lamb was slain, the son was then able to reproduce Himself through belief in His works. That reproduction is called the Holy Spirit. Through the Holy Spirit, humanity is able to enter into heaven as sons of God, and not servants. Everyone has an eternal being living inside of their bodies. For some, this being is the son of the Most High, and for others it is a disembodied spirit that will be lost forever. You are not your thoughts, emotions or your body. There is a greater being that lives within you, and that is the real you.

This being that lives within you is directly connected with the highest level of heaven. This being knows the truth, but it has not brought the mind and body into submission. The mind remains unchecked, so it steals the identity of the entire being and exalts itself. The mind is a very demanding entity. Without obedience, the mind will join forces with the body and together they will reproduce hell. Unless the higher being gains control of the thoughts of the mind, as well as the body, the higher being will not make it back into the divine presence. Knowledge of the truth is the only way to win the battle with the body and the mind. I'm not referring to head knowledge; I'm referring to that deep knowledge within known as the Lord's voice. Jesus says that His sheep hear His voice and they know Him. To hear the Lord's voice is to have an unshakable knowledge of the truth beyond reason. The mind loves to reason. It loves to gather information in order to inflate its own being. This is why it is hard for the highly educated to make it into heaven-they rely too much on their minds. The truth of the Most High cannot be learned with reason, but experience. You know the truth when you hear it, but the mind will try to reason it away. To silence to mind is a difficult thing to do if you don't feed the inner man. Thinking is very effective when it comes to matters of the body, but it is useless when it comes to spiritual things. While the mind is a higher being than the flesh, it is far lower that the spirit man. The spiritual existence is a much more complicated place than the physical world. In the highest realms of the spirit, there is no room for doubt. You have known things with certainty. The problem with the mind is that it knows very little, but it pretends to know so much. Every so many years, school text books are being revised to correct information that it claimed to be factual in the previous edition. Evolution has yet to be proven, but it is still taught to be indisputable fact. The mind is blind and it needs a guide. The folly of mankind is that we try to use the body to guide the mind, and vice versa. The mind and the body can only be controlled by the spirit man within. If you have not been born from on High, you will never gain control of your mind. The world around us is a construct of the human mind. We have tried to use our minds to solve humanity's problems, but the mind IS humanity's problem. The more and more we operate on the level of mind, the worse and worse our world becomes. This is the primary reason for the world's end. We think that we know it all, so we live as if we really do. As a result mankind is filled with man-made disasters. Scientific experimentation has been a great tragedy to the human condition. Primal beings thought with their minds, this is where we get the idea of the "survival of the fittest." Mind creates fear, hatred, jealousy and envy. It creates paranoia inside of its host. Paranoia breeds violence and intolerance. It is the mind that created war, racism, sexism, and perversions. The mind is the enemy of the true man. In order to bring thoughts into captivity, we must only allow our minds to think about the things that are true at the moment. Christ is the "I am" inside of man. If your thoughts go beyond what is, then you have lost control of your mind. To think properly is not to think about what could be or what was, it is to think about what is. The present moment is all you are guaranteed to have, so all of your thoughts should be focused on that moment. The bible says that sufficient for the day are the things thereof. To dwell on things that have not yet happened is too dangerous.

The mind loves to masquerade as being one with the body. In its own right, the mind is the god of the body. It can force the body to do things that are uncomfortable and unhealthy for the body. The mind is also able to reason the body out of doing things that it doesn't want to do. Simply thinking about eating food can cause the body to overeat. The body can feel to be full, but the mind can override that physical sensation and convince the body to eat more. The mind loves to force the body to over-do-it on just about anything. Consuming large amounts of alcohol is normally the product of the mind. The body knows that it has had enough to drink, but the mind isn't satisfied with the consumption-it wants more. This mental over consumption is due to the minds inability to feel satisfied. The mind is a creature that doesn't feel anything but hunger for control. It is a lost being that needs guidance from the deeper spirit. If there is no guidance the mind can cause serious problems. In fact, the mind is the point of entry for unclean spirits. Around each individual there is a cloud of energy called the spiritual atmosphere. Within this atmosphere are a variety of unclean spirits, injecting their thoughts and objectives into your life. If you cannot control your mind you will carry out the objective of these unclean spirits. No thought that you have originates from yourself. They are all external influences. The only thing that originates from you, are the things that you know from the inner man. These are the facts of life. For too long, we have been taught that we are "thinking beings", and that the mind is the divine aspect of our beings. The truth be told, the mind has done a lot to keep the human from evolving. The mind is very deceptive in leading people to believe that they have some form of control over it. The fact of the matter is that the mind fights back against people trying to control it. The mind wants to control itself. It isn't until we gain awareness in our spirits, that we are able to control the mind. This is the toughest spiritual battle that man can engage in. The flesh has its desires but the mind is a more formidable foe. The body can be controlled using narcotics or alcohol, or in some cases, sleep. The mind functions through all of the stimulants. Even in our dreams do our minds are functioning. It's no coincidence that we dream what we dream. Our minds are projecting its desires into our consciousness. The time of sleep is when the mind has its most freedom. During this time, the consciousness goes to a higher spiritual dimension, allowing the body to become revitalized. As the consciousness goes to a higher level, the mind conspires with the body to cause problems. This is the basis of our spiritual warfare. We must gain control over our minds, as well as our bodies. There is very little that goes on in terms of external warfare because the combat is with ourselves. Our spirits are fighting a life-long battle with the mind and the body. I'm not a person to criticize pastors and teachers, but it is my duty to speak the truth. The true nature of the mind is not properly taught in today's church, and we are suffering the consequences of it. Most people will fall away from the truth because they are waiting for a supernatural rapture to take place. This escapist mentality has caused many people to become weary in their fight to control or "subdue" the mind and the body. They figure that they are just going to be taken away before they have to confront their failure. Only those who accomplish this feat will enter the kingdom of heaven. There is actually work to be done on this earth that will continue for the rest of our lives. This is the measuring stick that the Lord is using to promote his people. Beyond this realm, is the realm of pure consciousness. Within that realm, there are even higher levels of consciousness called the heavens. This is only given to people who are successful in their fleshly endeavor of conquering the powers of the world known as the mind and the body. If one fails to overcome the world of the mind and the body, they will be cast into a state of eternal confusion known as hell.

Beyond consciousness of spirit is a realm of darkness called hell. For many people, darkness simply means the absence of light, but for the spiritually awake, darkness also means spiritual ignorance. The worst form of ignorance is spiritual or unconscious ignorance. In this state, the spirit is unaware that it is a spiritual being separate from the body, but it believes that it IS the body. When someone dies in this state, they will fight tooth and nail to hold on to the life of their bodies. The spirit is so unaware of its true nature that it is afraid of not having a body to occupy. The lure of bodily life is so strong that the spirit locks itself inside of the body and the mind. The spirit literally becomes a prisoner of the mind and the body. The natural process of death is for the inner man to enter deeper into the inner universe of the spirit. Once this happens, the spirit is freed from all of the pull of the external universe. For the spiritually dead, their spirit is unable to leave the material realm, and they are locked inside of the world of blood, organs, disease, decay and death. The only difference is that they cannot die twice physically. Hell is the inside of a body. It's the shrinking of the consciousness to the level of an atom, and that atom decays with the death of the body. With this death, the mind constructs a reality that is never-ending. The stay in hell is eternal because the mind no longer has the ability to be controlled. Form many people who claim of near death experiences, they describe the smell of hell to the smells of decaying flesh, vomit, and feces. All of these smells originate within the human body. The consciousness is the highest form of spirit, but when it fails to come to knowledge of itself it turns into a slave of mind and body. It loses its ability to rise above, so it sinks below. Hell is terrifying because there is no escape. The spirit has chosen fleshly life over spiritual life, so it will decay with the flesh. The decay is a never-ending event, which the spirit will endure forever. Many people have a difficult time comprehending the idea of eternal torment because we are small pieces of time itself. Outside of this life, there are no hours, minutes, days, weeks or years, there is only the present moment. The Almighty does not send anyone to hell, the soul that goes there has chosen its own fate. The hellish nature of our world is a reflection of the nature of the mind. Once the mind completes its creation, the end result will be hell. Man chooses to enter into a state of hell by his actions. This is why the bible emphasizes that God will not be mocked. The road to hell is just as clear as the road to heaven. Perfection of understanding is the key to avoiding a hellish nature in the next life.

For many people, perfection is a state that is completely unattainable for the human being. They believe that all humans are flawed, and that is the reason why it is impossible to be perfect. What they fail to realize is that they can never be perfect in the flesh, due to all of their past sins. The body has to constantly be subdued into proper behavior because it knows only the desires of itself. This is the basis for the sin body. The human body is nothing more than an animal like vessel, capable of holding a piece of the spirit of God within itself. Without the spirit, the body is dumb, and it seeks to satisfy animal-like desires. Once the body tastes sin, it is programmed to do the works of darkness. The body can be washed with baptism, but the core of it is still darkness. The stain of sin remains engrained within the DNA of the flesh. The desires of the flesh remain, even after baptism. For these reasons, the body can never be perfect. Although the body cannot be perfected, the spirit can. I'm not referring to the mind, because the mind can wander off into thoughts of darkness and confusion at any given time. No, the mind can never be perfected either. I'm referring to the inner man of the consciousness. Once that man is awakened, or born, it cannot sin because sin is the result of conscious unconsciousness. Sin is the rejection of the knowledge of God, or the higher self. Once a person is awakened in their spirit, as long as they live a life aware of that beings existence, they won't sin. But, if a person is awakened in their inner man and choose to ignore him, they not only sin, but they sin until death. The book of Hebrews speaks of people who have tasted of the heavenly gifts, but have chosen to turn away, for those people there is no hope for forgiveness. Jesus Christ came to the earth fully aware of who he was, and he never denied it. Because of this, he never sinned. He died in this perfect state, and that is the reason why he is the only way to the father. No other man has been born aware of who he was, and never forgot it or ignored it. No one! Once we enter into the knowledge of Christ, we have the ability to never forget it as well. Many people have chosen to live in a state of ignoring the truth, but they are aware of their higher self. For these people, hell awaits. The flesh blinds them to reality, and eventually, the Lord will give them over to their reprobate mind. This teaching is becoming more and more common amongst the believers of God, but the modern church is doing everything it can to demonize such teachings. This should make people wonder about the nature of these teachings. Many people are not aware of the dangers of false teachings and harlotry. They simply believe that a belief in God and Jesus is all they need, but they forget that the devils also believe, and tremble.

Now that I have given you some basic information about this life and the next, I want to take this opportunity to explain how our world is set up according to the spiritual realm. Within our planet are multiple realms or dimensions of existence. Within these dimensions there are beings of energy who exist on different energy frequencies. We as human beings exist on a frequency that allows us to only see and understand things that also exist on this frequency. I won't get into all of the science and physics behind how molecules vibrate at certain speeds to give the appearance of solidity, because there are ample books to explain this. What I want you to understand is how these realms interact with each other, and how this interaction affects you. As low frequency beings, we are bound to things that are similar to ourselves. This is why it is so hard for humans to comprehend the idea of spirit and eternity. We are material beings that are bound to the slavery of time. Within our dimension, we have internal clocks that measure our physical growth and development. We are only able to measure things that are within our realm, or our bubble. As human beings look towards the clouds, we are able to quantify our smallness in the universe. The oceans, mountains, trees and animals are placed around us so that we can correctly understand how the world around us can destroy us at any given time. Apart from physical size, humans are also threatened by microscopic organisms that can bring illnesses into our bodies. These physical limitations are placed around mankind in order to make us realize the vulnerability of our physical vessels. When it comes to the nature of the planet, the human body is frail and weak. The one thing that man has over his environment is his ability to think and create. We are able to isolate ourselves from the dangers around us through architecture and medicine. Man has manipulated his environment to the point that we feel secure within our existence. This false sense of security has blinded man to the fact that we were placed in this inferior position to force us to search for strength beyond our bodies. To a large degree we have, through the usage of our minds.

As I mentioned earlier, the mind has done a lot to control man and convince him that his true nature is not physical but mental. I also mentioned that the thoughts of the mind are not of the human being, but from the spiritual atmosphere around man. This atmosphere is comprised of the spiritual entities or energies that we have given the okay to communicate with us. You see, the human frequency is the lowest frequency in all of creation. We are on the outer edges of heaven and earth; therefore we are extremely vulnerable to the influences of higher energy beings. We were not given the ability to think for ourselves because we were designed to be the most like God. As humans, we are required by spiritual law to listen and receive instruction from another realm. Unfortunately for us, we have chosen to take orders from beings that are out to destroy our beings.

There are three realms of existence, but there are multiple dimensions within these realms. The first realm is the physical realm or the realm of matter. This is the current human realm. The members of this realm are bound to this realm only. We are unable to manipulate matter to the point that we are able to alter our appearances. We look how we are going to look, unless we go through some type of painful event to alter that state such as injury or surgery. We are very vulnerable to weather and atmospheric conditions for our survival. Without proper nutrition, our frail bodies will perish and decay. Within this realm there are other types of flesh. This can be seen through the multiple types of animals and organisms that exist on our planet. These beings are also subject to the "laws of nature." Beyond our planet there are other beings of flesh who are different than we are because they are able to survive in a variety of atmospheres. These beings are not within our solar system, despite what the conspiracy theorist may say. There are billions and billions of planets within our universe, and only a fool would say that none of them are inhabited. Despite their differences from us, they are still creatures of death. Everything that cannot live outside of the protection of some type of atmosphere is bound to physical death. Our current universe is all based upon matter. Every planet that we are able to see with our physical eyes, this includes telescopes, are of the same substance and destiny. We are bound to the laws of matter. These laws are called the laws of physics. Although the laws change from planet to planet, each planet has its own set of physical laws. Beings of higher frequencies are able to infiltrate our realm. They are able to influences the inhabitants of our realm by manipulating the circumstances of our realm. It is no accident that our society is taking the direction that it is taking. While many humans may feel that we are orchestrating our own futures, we are not. All of our history has been planned for us and we are only taking part in the final production. These beings exist in what is called the second heaven or atmospherean realm. This realm lies just outside of our universe and well beyond the furthest planet in our cosmic array. It may be difficult to believe that our universe has an end point, but it does. Everything that can be measured in timed distances is bound to have an end. It is well known that there exists a vacuum in space. This vacuum is pulling things in one general direction. The direction of the force is driving all of the visual creation into the atmospherean realm. This realm is filled with creatures that are mere images of the physical realm. These beings can only feel negative energies such as hate, envy, rage, jealousy, and strife. These energies act as food for their beings. Many of these creatures are what we know as demons, devils, fallen angels and unclean spirits. They were initially created to dwell in the third realm, but they became fascinated with their own being. They did not want to be submissive, but they wanted beings to submit to them. Although they are not intelligent beings, they are more knowledgeable than spiritually dead humans. These beings have the ability to come into our realm and make themselves visible to those who open themselves up to them. They are beastly in appearance, although they can appear beautiful in material forms. I hesitate to use terms such as reptilian because of its connotation, but many of them appear to reptile like creatures. Most of them appear as deformed shadows, but many of them have the ability to shape-shift into different appearances. They have to shift their appearance because they lack the ability to stay in one form for an extended period of time. Because they are simply energies, they cannot take on permanent form. Because they have been cut off from the life of the highest realm, they have to feed on whatever they can, and in most instances what they feed on human fear. Just as beings of DNA have to ingest other forms of DNA for survival, these beings of negative energy have to ingest other forms of negative energy in order to survive. Without human iniquities, these beings would not exist. They cannot create energies for themselves, so they had to created beings that can produce negative energy for them to feed off of. For this reason, humanity was created.

It is a great taboo to insinuate that the human body was not created by the Almighty God, but evidence shows that it wasn't. God created the inner man, or the spirit man to inhabit the bodies. The bodies were made by lower forms of spirit beings as vessels of survival. They knew that they did not have the ability to live without bodies; they manipulated matter in order to have something to live in. Because of their spiritual nature (higher than human, but lower than God) they could not put all of themselves into the human body. Once they occupied the body, they were only able to stay inside of them for a short time before they had to leave them. They were also not able to move or control the bodies because there nature is only mind. They were able to see through the eyes and hear through the ears, but they had no control of the body. No one knows how many bodies were made, but there could have been many. God, knowing their plans, placed His Spirits inside of the bodies in the form of Adam and Eve. The mind is the presence of these lower beings, while the Spirit is the presence of God. Jesus Christ says that he is the resurrection. At the moment of Adam and Eve's entrance into the human body, all of the bodies that were made by the second class of beings came to life. They only had minds, and the breath of life, but not the Spirit. It was Adam and Eve's job to teach these beings the ways of the most high, but they failed. They allowed the enemy to lead them into the state or condition of sin. Sin is not an act or deed, but it is a state of being. Once Adam and Eve partook in the will that was not of God, they became sinners. The spirit was taken from them and they were forced to become beings of only mind and body. This act also gave the second class of beings the right to inhabit these bodies through the actions of the mind. To be possessed is to be controlled by thought and mind. Every human being that is controlled by the thoughts of the mind, are in some way, possessed. None of the bodies of the first beings we created through birth.

Because of this they could not be occupied and controlled by the lower dark spirits. After Adam and Eve's fall, humanity was now created through sexual conception and birth. Through birth, the unclean spirits have access to the human body through the acts of iniquity. It is this iniquity that feeds their very existence. For this reason, Jesus Christ had to be born of a woman, to redeem those also born of women.

The life of the flesh is a complicated existence. Because the physical body is the lowest form of being, we have to fight off many attacks from higher forms of beings. These beings are located in the atmospheres of our planets; this is why they are called atmospherean beings. It is no coincidence that we live in a world that is surrounded by an atmosphere that not only keeps us alive, but has the ability to kill us if we try to pass through it. It is difficult to explain how this works because it's something that has to be revealed to you. The atmospherean realm is located just outside of our universe. All of the occupied space of our outer universe is considered to be a part of the second realm. Humanity has no reason to journey into the reaches of outer space because there is nothing for our being out there. The atmospherean beings are dark energies that surround us on all sides. For spirits who fail to come to the knowledge of themselves, they will be dissolved into this realm. They will be dissolved into the substance of outer space and sent from planet to planet before the resurrection. The dark beings of this realm have no interest in the well-being of the human beings. They only want to feed off of our iniquities, while trying to piggyback a way into the highest realm. You see, many of these beings want to get out of their miserable existence in their realm. They want to return to the glories of the Lords presence, but they are forbidden to. They want to not only control your mind, but drain it of all knowledge of the things of God. This is why it's so important that you don't store knowledge within the recesses of the mind, but deeper within the nature of the inner being. We are living in hostile territory on all sides. The dark beings of the second heaven are larger and darker than we can imagine. Some of them are large enough to cover entire continents of our planet, while others are smaller than a small cat. They vary in appearance and motives. As long as humans are limited by the abilities of our physical eyes, we will never truly understand what the beings look like. They are motivated by hatred and fear and they seek to keep humans in bondage to their minds and bodies.

Beyond this realm exists what is called the realm of light and life. For many people this is called heaven, for others it is known as something else. Within this realm resides the highest concentration of the presence of the Father. The presence is so high in fact, that nothing other than like substances can reside there. If you can imagine our dark universe as an orb placed inside of a huge room of white light, this would give you an idea of the construction of the three realms. Once a conscious being enters this realm, their size and stature becomes unquantifiable. There is a huge misconception about the nature of beings and their journey to heaven. First off, we don't GO to heaven; heaven absorbs us into its substance. The book of revelation says that the New Jerusalem "comes down" out of heaven. Secondly, nothing really exists in this realm. The bible says that heaven and earth shall pass away as a scroll. This tells us that there is nothing that is solid or non-changing in this realm. Lastly, God does not reside in heaven, heaven resides in God. The Lord of all is the very nature of heaven itself. He has the ability to make this realm whatever He wants it to be for us. If you've ever seen the first Matrix movie, it would be similar to the giant white room that Morpheus took Neo into. Within the highest realm exists all things, yet nothing really exists there. This is how the New Jerusalem can come out of heaven. The Lord creates the New Jerusalem out of all potential; in essence, He creates an entirely new realm. This realm radiates with love, because God is love. Because of the vastness and endlessness of the third heaven, the New Jerusalem will be larger than all of the inhabitable planets of our universe combined. In its very essence, the New Heaven will be the creation of a new dimension. Within this dimension will live all of the spirits that came to knowledge of themselves while living in the body. No one knows what the new forms will appear as, but they will not be flesh and blood. We will become the highest forms of beings in all of creation. Because we were created and placed inside of bodies, our consciousness will always be aware of itself, therefore we will always exist. After this point, we are only able to speculate about what God has planned for us. There are many things that the Lord has kept to Himself and we can do nothing more than wait and see.

www.ingramcontent.com/pod-product-compliance
Lightning Source LLC
Chambersburg PA
CBHW051848040426
42447CB00006B/752